PRETTY NATURE GIRLS

GRAYSCALE GIRLS COLLECTION

BOOK 1

Tips & Suggestions

This grayscale coloring book is different than a traditional line art coloring book. You'll notice there's already shading with light and dark gray tones. When you color over the shading, you'll instantly create more depth. This will make your picture come to life with realistic, three dimensional effects.

To remove the page cut along the dotted line.

Here are some quick tips for beginners:

Not sure? Practice first. When using coloring tools for the first time, create a separate little test page (swatch) to test how the color looks and to practice heavy and light strokes.

Coloring Tip: Use a circular motion to create a smoother effect (a blunter pencil tip is better for this than a sharp tip). Also test out this book's paper by coloring the mini-pictures at the front and back of the book.

Avoid using very dark, heavy colors on top of light grayscale shading. Start by using a light or medium color to let the shading show through, then add darker colors to achieve the effect you desire.

Layer & Blend Colors: First start with light colors and press lightly. Then layer and blend using medium and darker colors and heavier strokes. Use lighter colors to soften and smooth dark strokes, or blend with a cotton swab, tissue, brush or blending pencil/pen. To create highlights, you can select lighter colors, use an eraser, leave areas white or use white or yellow markers.

Use a Blotting Page: To ensure that no ink seeps through, put a piece of cardboard or thick paper behind the page you're coloring (or remove page first before coloring).

Choosing Your Tools: Use a combination of colored pencils, gel pens, watercolor pencils, chalk pastels or marker pens. Markers can be water or alcohol based. Beginner-grade supplies can be used, although artist quality is recommended if your budget allows. Artist quality brands cost more, but create smoother, brighter results and last longer.

Not sure about tools and techniques? Search online for product reviews of pencils, markers etc. and how-to videos and blogs about blending and shading techniques.

Also check out **YouTube** for detailed tutorial videos about basic & advanced techniques of grayscale coloring, shading, highlighting and layering.

Thank you for choosing this grayscale coloring book.

We wish you an amazing coloring session!

With  from Nougu Art

Nougu
COLORING ART

Get a FREE coloring pack (PDF download)

when you join our newsletter

nougubooks.com/free

Pretty Nature Girls, Grayscale Girls Collection Book 1
My First Grayscale Coloring Book for Girls & Adults
1st English Edition

Printed and published by BoD – Books on Demand, Norderstedt, Germany
ISBN: 9783748192848

Design: Nougu Art Coloring, a division of NouguBooks.com
All other artist graphics used by permission under Creative Commons license CC0

For all other inquires contact us at: hello@nougubooks.com

For free coloring pages, tips and book announcements visit us at www.nougubooks.com

LET'S GO!
It's a Crazy Coloring Warm Up!

COME ON!

WORK THOSE COLORS!

Here are
two bonus
coloring pages
for you!

I LOVE YOU

A cute girl from
"Pretty Nature Girls"
Book 2

A pretty girl from
"Dream Girls of Grayscale"
Book 3

I LOVE YOU

Other Books in Our Collections

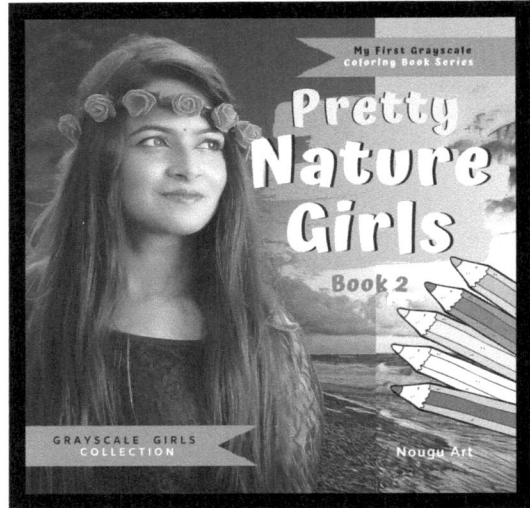

Upcoming Collections

Light Fantasy, Gothic and Steampunk
Cats and Dogs, Coloring for Guys & Boys

Be a Part of Nougu Art

Join our newsletter for exclusive freebies.
Be the first to know about new book launches,
get special deals! Visit our website for free
downloads, links, inspiration galleries, meet
the furface behind the brand and more...

Instagram
@Nougu.Books

Website
www.NouguBooks.com

Etsy Shop
etsy.com/shop/MaisonNougat